Handy Nebraska Genealogy Handbook

Gary L. Morris

©2015 Gary L. Morris

ISBN-13: 978-1507836897

ISBN-10: 1507836899

Table of Contents

Notes

Genealogical Research in Nebraska

There are many genealogical records and resources available for tracing your family history in Nebraska. Because there are so many records held at many different locations, tracking down the records for your ancestor can be a difficult task. Don't worry though, we know just where they are, and we'll show you which records you'll need, while helping you to understand:

1. What they are
2. Where to find them
3. How to use them

These records can be found both online and off, so we'll introduce you to online websites, indexes and databases, as well as brick-and-mortar repositories and other institutions that will help with your research in Nebraska. So that you will have a more comprehensive understanding of these records, we have provided a brief history of the "Cornhusker State" to illustrate what type of records may have been generated during specific time periods. That information will assist you in pinpointing times and locations on which to focus the search for your Nebraska ancestors and their records.

A Brief History of Nebraska

The Native American tribes that inhabited Nebraska upon the arrival of white settlers in the 18th century consisted of the Omaha, Oto, Pawnee, and Ponca, along with several other nomadic groups. The Indians developed friendly relations with the French and Spanish explorers traveling through Nebraska en route to the west via the Missouri River. Both Spain and France claimed the area, though at the time of the Louisiana Purchase in 1803, the region was a French Territory.

White settlement west of the Mississippi River was forbidden by the Indian Intercourse Act of 1834, but nothing prevented whites from traversing the area. Many did between 1840 and 1866, as the area provided a natural thoroughfare to the west. The Oregon, Mormon, and California trails all passed through Nebraska, and a system of forts was established along each of those routes to protect travelers from attacks by local Native Americans.

Nebraska Territory, which stretched from Kansas to Canada and from the Missouri River to the Rocky Mountains, was established by the Kansas-Nebraska Act of 1854. With the creation of the territory however, came increased conflict between the white settlers and the Native American tribes. Indians were forced to cede more and more of their land, and during the 1860's and 1870's western Nebraska was a battleground for Indians and US soldiers. The Indians were defeated by 1890, and transferred to reservations in Nebraska itself, Oklahoma, and South Dakota.

With the defeat of the Indians settlement increased rapidly. The Homestead Act of 1862 had promised settlers 160 acres of land at a nominal fee, and with the threat of Indian violence removed, many from the eastern United States and Europe snapped up the land on offer. The railroads further accelerate immigration to the area, many of whom were Union veterans who bolstered the Republican dominance and furthered the cause for statehood. Nebraska was granted statehood on March 1, 1867, and soon developed as a center for farming and ranching.

Important Dates in Nebraska History

1803 - Part of Louisiana Purchase

1804 - Lewis and Clark traveled up the Missouri River

1819 - U.S. Army established Fort Atkinson

1823 - First permanent white settlement built at Bellevue

1833 - U.S. government purchases Pawnee Indian lands south of the Platte River

1854 - Becomes a separate territory

1862 - Homestead Act attracts new settlers from the east into Nebraska

1867 – Statehood

1868 - Lincoln replaces Omaha as state capitol

1877 - Famed Indian warrior Crazy Horse surrenders along with 1,000 of his followers

Famous Battles Fought in Nebraska

There were no Civil War battles fought in Nebraska, but there were many bloody clashes with Native American tribes between 1855 and 1876. The most important of those clashes are listed below with links to the battle accounts.

These battle accounts that exist can be very effective in uncovering the military records of your ancestor. They can tell you what regiments fought in which battles, and often include the names and ranks of many officers and enlisted men.

Battle of Ash Hollow, 1855: http://www.legendsofamerica.com/ne-indianbattles.html#Blue Water Battle

Battle of Mud Springs, 1865: http://www.legendsofamerica.com/ne-indianbattles3.html

Battle of Massacre Canyon, 1873: http://www.nebraskahistory.org/publish/publicat/history/full-text/NH1973Massacre_Cnyn.pdf

Common Nebraska Genealogical Issues and Resources to Overcome Them

Boundary Changes: Boundary changes are a common obstacle when researching Nebraska ancestors. You could be searching for an ancestor's record in one county when in fact it is stored in a different one due to historical county boundary changes.

The **Atlas of Historical County Boundaries** can help you to overcome that problem. It provides a chronological listing of every boundary change that has occurred in the history of Nebraska.

Atlas of Historical County Boundaries:
http://publications.newberry.org/ahcbp/documents/NE_Consolidated _Chronology.htm#Consolidated_Chronology

Name Changes: Surname changes, variations, and misspellings can complicate genealogical research. It is important to check all spelling variations. Soundex, a program that indexes names by sound, is a useful first step, but you can't rely on it completely as some name variations result in different Soundex codes. The surnames could be different, but the first name may be different too. You can also find records filed under initials, middle names, and nicknames as well, so you will need to **get creative with surname variations** and spellings in order to cover all the possibilities. For help with surname variations read our instructional article on **How to Use Soundex**.

get creative with surname variations:
http://obituarieshelp.org/blog/?p=634

How to Use Soundex: http://obituarieshelp.org/blog/?p=505

Nebraska Genealogical Organizations and Archives

Genealogical resources include not only records, but the organizations that house them, or can direct you to them. These institutions include: *Archives, Libraries, Genealogical Societies, Family History Centers, Universities, Churches, and Museums.*

Following are links to their websites, their physical addresses, and a summary of the records you can find there.

Archives and Libraries

Nebraska State Historical Society Library and Archives - military history, land records, Indian affairs, census, immigration records, marriages and divorces, taxes, elections, civil and criminal suits, naturalization proceedings, church records, business records

Library/Archives
Nebraska State Historical Society
1500 "R" Street
Lincoln, NE 68501
Telephone: 402-471-4751
Fax: 402-471-3100

Mailing Address:
P.O. Box 82554
Lincoln, NE 68501

Nebraska State Historical Society Library and Archives:
http://www.nebraskahistory.org/lib-arch/index.shtml

Lincoln City Libraries – wide variety of genealogical records and resources

Lincoln City Libraries:
http://www.lincolnlibraries.org/webliographies/Genealogy_Resource
s.htm

National Archives—Central Plains Region (Kansas City) –
census, military records, pension and bounty-land warrant
applications

400 West Pershing Road
Kansas City, MO 64108
Telephone: 816-268-8000

National Archives—Central Plains Region:
http://www.archives.gov/kansas-city/public/

Omaha Public Library – town and county histories, maps and
gazetteers, pioneer memoirs, Omaha-area school yearbooks, church
and parish histories, Douglas County birth, death, and marriage
registers, Index to Naturalizations in Nebraska and Some Iowa
Counties, 1906 and Prior, cemetery records, Nebraska periodicals

215 S. 15th Street
Omaha, NE 68102
Tel: 402-444-4833 or 402-444-4844

Omaha Public Library:
http://guides.omahalibrary.org/content.php?pid=95140&sid=832031

Nebraska Genealogical and Historical Societies

Genealogical and historical societies have access to extensive catalogues of genealogical data. They are also able to offer expert guidance for genealogical researchers. Many members are professional genealogists who are most willing to share their expertise in finding ancestors.

Greater Omaha Genealogy Society – surname directory, research assistance, online vital records indices, newsletter

P.O. Box 4011
Omaha, NE 68104

Greater Omaha Genealogy Society:
http://gogsmembers.wordpress.com/

Douglas County Historical Society - Douglas County vital records, naturalization records, historical newspapers, diaries, letters, organizational records, and more

Library/Archives Center
Historic Fort Omaha
5730 N 30th Street, #11A
Omaha, NE 68111
Tel: 402-451-1013
email:archivist@omahahistory.org

Douglas County Historical Society:
http://www.omahahistory.org/collections.html

Nebraska State Genealogical Society - family histories, city and county histories, vital records indices, yearbooks, ethnic records, censuses, and more

P.O. Box 5608
Lincoln, NE 68505-0608

Nebraska State Genealogical Society: http://nesgs.org/

Nebraska State Genealogical Society Library (Beatrice Public Library)

100 N. 16th St.
Beatrice, NE 68310.

Nebraska State Genealogical Society Library:
http://www.beatrice.ne.gov/library/

Nebraska Mailing Lists

Mailing lists are internet based facilities that use email to distribute a single message to all who subscribe to it. When information on a particular surname, new records, or any other important genealogy information related to the mailing list topic becomes available, the subscribers are alerted to it. Joining a mailing list is an excellent way to stay up to date on Nebraska genealogy research topics. Rootsweb have an extensive listing of **Nebraska Mailing Lists** on a variety of topics.

Nebraska Mailing Lists:
http://lists.rootsweb.ancestry.com/index/usa/NE/misc.html

Nebraska Message Boards

A message board is another internet based facility where people can post questions about a specific genealogy topic and have it answered by other genealogists. If you have questions about a surname, record type, or research topic, you can post your question and other researchers and genealogists will help you with the answer. Be sure to check back regularly, as the answers are not emailed to you. The Nebraska message boards at **Rootsweb** are completely free to use.

Rootsweb:
http://boards.rootsweb.com/localities.northam.usa.states/mb.ashx

Nebraska Newspapers and Periodicals

Many genealogy periodicals and historical newspapers contain reprinted copies of family genealogies, transcripts of family Bible records, information about local records and archives, census indexes, church records, queries, land records, obituaries, court records, cemetery records, and wills. The following sites have historical Nebraska newspapers and periodicals that you can search online or on-site.

Omaha Public Library – local newspapers on microfilm dating back to the 1850s, periodicals

215 S. 15th Street
Omaha, NE 68102
Tel: 402-444-4833 or 402-444-4844

Omaha Public Library:
http://guides.omahalibrary.org/content.php?pid=95140&sid=712112

Douglas County Historical Society – large collection of newspapers dating from 1857 to circa 2004

Library/Archives Center
Historic Fort Omaha
5730 N 30th Street, #11A
Omaha, NE 68111
Tel: 402-451-1013
email:archivist@omahahistory.org

Douglas County Historical Society:
http://www.omahahistory.org/news.html

GenealogyBank.com – free searchable database of Nebraska newspaper archives, 1868–1983

GenealogyBank.com:
http://www.genealogybank.com/gbnk/newspapers/explore/USA/Nebraska/

Library of Congress Digital Newspaper Directory – free searchable database of historical U.S. newspapers dating from 1690-present

Library of Congress Digital Newspaper Directory: http://chroniclingamerica.loc.gov/search/titles/

The Online Books Page – links to historical Nebraska books and periodicals available for viewing online, dating from mid-16th century

The Online Books Page link to: http://onlinebooks.library.upenn.edu

NewspaperArchive.com – largest online database of historical newspapers in the world.

NewspaperArchive.com: http://newspaperarchive.com/

Historical Nebraska Maps and Gazetteers

Maps are an integral part of genealogical research. They help us to
locate landmarks, towns, cities, parishes, states, provinces,
waterways and roads and streets. They also help us to determine
when and where boundary changes might have taken place, and give
us a visualization of the area we're researching in.

For locating place names, a gazetteer is the best possible resource for
any genealogist. Gazetteers are also sometimes called "place name
dictionaries", and can help you to locate the area in which you need
to conduct research. Below are links to the maps and gazetteers for
research in Nebraska.

Peabody GNIS Service – Nebraska:
http://peabody.research.yale.edu/cgi-
bin/Query.GNIS?ST=Nebraska&SU=1

Color Landform Atlas – Nebraska:
http://fermi.jhuapl.edu/states/ne_0.html

1985 U.S. Atlas: http://www.livgenmi.com/1895/NE/

Nebraska Hometown Locator:
http://nebraska.hometownlocator.com/

Nebraska City Directories

.
City directories are similar to telephone directories in that they list the residents of a particular area. The difference though is what is important to genealogists, and that is they pre-date telephone directories. You can find an ancestor's information such as their street address, place of employment, occupation, or the name of their spouse. A one-stop-shop for finding city directories in Nebraska is the **Nebraska Online Historical Directories** which contains a listing of every available online historical directory related to Nebraska.

Nebraska Online Historical Directories:
https://sites.google.com/site/onlinedirectorysite/Home/usa/ne

Douglas County Historical Society – miscellaneous Nebraska City Directories, 1866-present

Library/Archives Center
Historic Fort Omaha
5730 N 30th Street, #11A
Omaha, NE 68111
Tel: 402-451-1013
email:archivist@omahahistory.org

Douglas County Historical Society:
http://www.omahahistory.org/genealogy.html

Nebraska Genealogical Records

Birth, Death, Marriage and Divorce Records – Also known as vital records, birth, death, and marriage certificates are the most basic, yet most important records attached to your ancestor. The reason for their importance is that they not only place your ancestor in a specific place at a definite time, but potentially connect the individual to other relatives. Below is a list of repositories and websites where you can find Nebraska vital records.

Nebraska Department of Health & Human Services – birth and death records, 1904-present; marriage and divorce certificates, 1909-present

Division of Public Health
Vital Records
P.O. Box 95065
Lincoln, NE 68509-5065
Phone: (402) 471-2871
E-mail:DHHS.VitalRecords@nebraska.gov

Nebraska Department of Health & Human Services:
http://dhhs.ne.gov/publichealth/pages/vitalrecords.aspx

Nebraska State Historical Society Library and Archives – marriage records for 86 of the state's 93 counties (often dating back to the county's origin), church records containing marriages, baptisms, births, and deaths

Library/Archives   Fax: 402-471-3100
Nebraska State Historical Society
1500 "R" Street   **Mailing Address**:
Lincoln, NE 68501   P.O. Box 82554
Telephone: 402-471-4751   Lincoln, NE 68501

Nebraska State Historical Society Library and Archives:
http://www.nebraskahistory.org/lib-arch/index.shtml

Omaha Public Library – town Douglas County birth, death, and marriage registers; births: 1874-1910, marriages: Aug. 22, 1856-March 30, 1941; Feb. 17, 1943-Dec. 30, 2005; Index: 1856-May 1932, deaths: 1873-1904; South Omaha Dec. 1895-July 1905; City of Omaha 1895-1915, marriage records for several other Nebraska counties on microfilm

215 S. 15th Street
Omaha, NE 68102
Tel: 402-444-4833 or 402-444-4844

Omaha Public Library:
http://guides.omahalibrary.org/content.php?pid=95140&sid=832031

Douglas County Historical Society - City of Omaha Death Records, 1873-1907; Douglas County Marriage Records, 1856-1932, Certificates from 1856-1912

Library/Archives Center
Historic Fort Omaha
5730 N 30th Street, #11A
Omaha, NE 68111
Tel: 402-451-1013
email:archivist@omahahistory.org

Douglas County Historical Society:
http://www.omahahistory.org/collections.html

Family Search has the following index which can be searched online for free:

Nebraska, Marriages, 1855-1995::
https://familysearch.org/search/collection/1708654

Census Reports

Census records are among the most important genealogical documents for placing your ancestor in a particular place at a specific time. Like BDM records, they can also lead you to other ancestors, particularly those who were living under the authority of the head of household.

Federal census records for Nebraska exist from 1860–1940 and can be found at:

Nebraska State Historical Society Library and Archives – Federal, state, city, and territorial census records from 1845-1940

Library/Archives
Nebraska State Historical Society
1500 "R" Street
Lincoln, NE 68501
Telephone: 402-471-4751
Fax: 402-471-3100

Mailing Address:
P.O. Box 82554
Lincoln, NE 68501

Nebraska State Historical Society Library and Archives:
http://www.nebraskahistory.org/lib-arch/services/refrence/la_pubs/census2.htm

National Archives—Central Plains Region (Kansas City) – Federal population censuses for all states 1790-1930

400 West Pershing Road
Kansas City, MO 64108
Telephone: 816-268-8000

National Archives—Central Plains Region:
http://www.archives.gov/kansas-city/public/

The **Free Census Project** has transcribed many Nebraska indexes and new material is added daily

Free Census Project: http://usgwcensus.org/cenfiles/ne.htm

Access Genealogy – Nebraska county census records from 1860-1930

Access Genealogy: http://www.accessgenealogy.com/census/nebraska-census-records.htm

African American Census Schedules Online – slave schedules, mortality schedules, slave-owners census

African American Census Schedules Online: http://www.afrigeneas.com/aacensus/ga/

Native Americans in Census Records (US National Archives): http://www.archives.gov/research/census/native-americans/

Nebraska Church Records

Church and synagogue records are a valuable resource, especially for baptisms, marriages, and burials that took place before 1900. You will need to at least have an idea of your ancestor's religious denomination, and in most cases you will have to visit a brick and mortar establishment to view them.

Most church records are kept by the individual church, although in some denominations, records are placed in a regional archive or maintained at the diocesan level. Local Historical Societies are sometimes the repository for the state's older church records. Below are links archives that maintain church records, as well as a few databases that can be viewed online.

The **Family History Library** contains many church records from a variety of denominations on microfilm.

Family History Library:
http://familysearch.org/learn/wiki/en/Family_History_Library

Nebraska State Historical Society Library and Archives – records of many Nebraska churches including: Catholic, Congregational, Lutheran, Presbyterian, Evangelical, Methodist, Baptist, United Church of Christ, and more

Library/Archives
Nebraska State Historical Society
1500 "R" Street
Lincoln, NE 68501
Telephone: 402-471-4751
Fax: 402-471-3100

Mailing Address:
P.O. Box 82554
Lincoln, NE 68501

Nebraska State Historical Society Library and Archives:
http://www.nebraskahistory.org/lib-arch/research/manuscripts/church/

Central Repositories for Denominational Records

Church of Jesus Christ of Latter-day Saints (Mormons)

Early Mormon Church records for Nebraska can be found on film located at the LDS Family History Library in Salt Lake City and can be searched via the **Family History Library Catalog**

Family History Library Catalog:
https://familysearch.org/eng/Library/FHLC/frameset_fhlc.asp

Lutheran

Archives of the Nebraska Synod
4980 South 118 Street, Suite D
Omaha, NE 68137-2220
Phone: (402) 896-5311
Fax: (402) 896-5354
E-mail: **office@nebraskasynod.org.**

Archives of the Nebraska Synod: http://www.nebraskasynod.org/

Methodist

Nebraska Wesleyan University
Historical Archives United Methodist Church
5000 St. Paul Avenue
Lincoln, NE 68504
Phone: (402) 465-2400
Fax: (402) 465-2189

Nebraska Wesleyan University Historical Archives United Methodist Church:
http://www.nebrwesleyan.edu/cochrane-woods-library/united-methodist-archives

Presbyterian

Presbyterian Historical Society
United Presbyterian Church in the U.S.
425 Lombard Street
Philadelphia, PA 19147
Phone: (215) 627-1852
Fax: (215) 627-0509

Presbyterian Historical Society: http://www.history.pcusa.org/

Roman Catholic

Diocese of Lincoln
P.O. Box 80328
Lincoln, NE 68501-0328
Phone: (402) 488-0921

Diocese of Lincoln:
http://www.dioceseoflincoln.org/Pages/default.aspx

Archdiocese of Omaha
100 North 62 Street
Omaha, NE 68132-2795
Phone: (402) 558-3100
Fax: (402) 558-3026

Archdiocese of Omaha: http://www.archomaha.org/

Nebraska Military Records

More than 40 million Americans have participated in some time of war service since America was colonized. The chance of finding your ancestor amongst those records is exceptionally high. Military records can even reveal individuals who never actually served, such as those who registered for the two World Wars but were never called to duty.

Below are a number of links to websites and archives that contain Nebraska military records.

Nebraska State Historical Society Library and Archives – records of Militia and Volunteer Units, 1855-1880; includes muster rolls, property lists, correspondence, reports, personnel and payroll lists and more

Library/Archives
Nebraska State Historical Society
1500 "R" Street
Lincoln, NE 68501
Telephone: 402-471-4751
Fax: 402-471-3100

Mailing Address:
P.O. Box 82554
Lincoln, NE 68501

Nebraska State Historical Society Library and Archives:
http://nebraskahistory.org/lib-arch/research/public/state_finding_aids/military_dept.pdf

US Department of Veterans Affairs Nationwide Gravesite Locator – includes information on veterans and their family members buried in veterans and military cemeteries having a government grave marker.

US Department of Veterans Affairs Nationwide Gravesite Locator: http://gravelocator.cem.va.gov/

You may also find your ancestor's military records in the following databases:

United States General Index to Pension Files, 1861-1934:
https://familysearch.org/search/collection/1919699

United States Index to Service Records, War with Spain, 1898:
https://familysearch.org/search/collection/1919583

United States Index to Indian Wars Pension Files, 1892-1926 – military pension records of soldiers who fought in the Indian Wars between 1817 and 1898

United States Index to Indian Wars Pension Files, 1892-1926:
https://familysearch.org/search/collection/1979427

United States Registers of Enlistments in the U.S. Army, 1798-1914 - index of men who enlisted in the United States Army, 1798-1914.

United States Registers of Enlistments in the U.S. Army, 1798-1914: https://familysearch.org/search/collection/1880762

United States Mexican War Pension Index, 1887-1926 - index to Mexican War pension files for service between 1846 and 1848

United States Mexican War Pension Index, 1887-1926:
https://familysearch.org/search/collection/1979390

Civil War Soldiers Service Records - Service records for both Union and Confederate soldiers indexed by soldier's name, rank, and unit.

Civil War Soldier Service Records:
http://go.fold3.com/civilwar_records/

Nebraska Cemetery Records

As convenient as it is to search cemetery records online, keep in mind that there are a few disadvantages over visiting a cemetery in person. They are:

1. Tombstone information is not always accurately transcribed
2. The arrangement of the graves in a cemetery can be crucial as family members are often buried next to each other or in the same grave. This arrangement is not always preserved in the alphabetical indexes that are found online.

With that information in mind, the following websites have databases that can be searched online for Nebraska Cemetery records.

Nebraska Gravestones Photo Project – over 250,000 gravestone photo records from across the state of Nebraska

Nebraska Gravestones Photo Project:
http://nebraskagravestones.org/

Nebraska Tombstone Transcription Project - death and burial records

Nebraska Tombstone Transcription Project:
http://www.usgwtombstones.org/nebraska/nebraska.html

African American Cemeteries Online – African American, slave, and Native American cemetery records

African American Cemeteries Online:
http://africanamericancemeteries.com/

Access Genealogy – huge database of Nebraska cemetery record transcriptions

Access Genealogy:
http://www.accessgenealogy.com/cemetery/nebraska-cemetery-records.htm

Find a Grave – over 100 million grave records can be searched on this site. Search can be conducted by name, location, or cemetery name.

Find a Grave: http://www.findagrave.com/

Interment.net - A free online database containing approximately 4 million cemetery records from around the world.

Interment.net: http://www.interment.net/

Billion Graves – as the name implies, you can search a billion records including headstone photos, transcriptions, cemetery records, and grave locations.

Billion Graves:
http://billiongraves.com/pages/search/index.php#cemetery

Nebraska Obituaries

Obituaries can reveal a wealth about our ancestor and other relatives. You can search our **Nebraska Newspaper Obituaries Listings** from hundreds of Nebraska newspapers online for free.

Nebraska Newspaper Obituaries Listings:
http://obituarieshelp.org/nebraska_newspaper_obituaries.html

Nebraska Wills and Probate Records

The documents found in a probate packet may include a complete inventory of a person's estate, newspaper entries, witness testimony, a copy of a will, list of debtors and creditors, names of executors or trustees, names of heirs. They can not only tell you about the ancestor you're currently researching, but lead to other ancestors.

Nebraska probate records have are kept by the **Clerks of the County Court**.

Clerks of the County Court: http://supremecourt.ne.gov/cc/clerks

Nebraska State Historical Society Library and Archives – county probate records dating from min 19th century

Library/Archives
Nebraska State Historical Society
1500 "R" Street
Lincoln, NE 68501
Telephone: 402-471-4751
Fax: 402-471-3100

Mailing Address:
P.O. Box 82554
Lincoln, NE 68501

Nebraska State Historical Society Library and Archives:
http://www.nebraskahistory.org/lib-arch/services/refrence/la_pubs/probate_guide.pdf

Nebraska Immigration and Naturalization Records

The naturalization process generated many types of records, including petitions, declarations of intention, and oaths of allegiance. These records can provide family historians with information such as a person's birth date and place of birth, immigration year, marital status, spouse information, occupation, witnesses' names and addresses, and more.

Nebraska State Historical Society Library and Archives – immigration and naturalization index 1906 and prior

Library/Archives
Nebraska State Historical Society
1500 "R" Street
Lincoln, NE 68501
Telephone: 402-471-4751
Fax: 402-471-3100

Mailing Address:
P.O. Box 82554
Lincoln, NE 68501

Nebraska State Historical Society Library and Archives
http://nebraskahistory.org/lib-
arch/services/refrence/la_pubs/natural3.htm

Douglas County Historical Society – Douglas County Declarations of Intention, 1867-1964; Petitions for Citizenship, 1881-1936

Library/Archives Center
Historic Fort Omaha
5730 N 30th Street, #11A
Omaha, NE 68111
Tel: 402-451-1013
email:archivist@omahahistory.org

Douglas County Historical Society:
http://www.omahahistory.org/genealogy.html

U.S. National Archives – Immigration and Naturalization records, 1787-1993

U.S. National Archives: http://www.archives.gov/research/guide-fed-records/groups/085.html

Nebraska Native American Records

Access Genealogy – Nebraska Native American census records, tribal histories, and much more

Access Genealogy:
http://www.accessgenealogy.com/native/nebraska-indian-tribes.htm

U.S. National Archives - information on American Indians who maintained their ties to Federally-recognized Tribes (1830-1970).

U.S. National Archives: http://www.archives.gov/research/native-americans/

Records of the Bureau of Indian Affairs (BIA):
http://www.archives.gov/research/guide-fed-records/groups/075.html

American Indians Records Repository - records dating from the 1700s including trust, education and other historic Indian Affairs records

American Indian Records Repository
Meritex Enterprises
17501 West 98th Street
Lenexa, KS 66219
Phone: 913-888-0601

American Indians Records Repository:
http://www.doi.gov/ost/records_mgmt/american-indian-records-repository.cfm

Missing Matriarchs – Resources for Researching Female Nebraska Ancestors

Looking for female ancestors requires an adjustment of how we view traditional records sources. A woman's identity was often under that of her husband, and often individual records for them can be difficult to locate. The following resources are effective in locating female ancestors in Nebraska where traditional records may not reveal them.

Bibliographies

1. *Schoolwomen of the Prairies and Plains: Personal Narratives from Iowa, Kansas, and Nebraska, 1860's – 1920,* Mary Hurlbut Cordier (University of New Mexico Press, 1997)
2. *Nebraska Quilts and Quiltmakers,* Patricia Cox Crewes (University of Nebraska Press, 1991)
3. *Agrarian Women: Wives and Mothers in Rural Nebraska,* Deborah Fink (University of North Carolina Press, 1992)
4. *Nebraska Women Through the Years, 1867-1967,* Governor's Commission on the Status of Women (Johnsen Publishing Co., 1967)

Selected Resources for Nebraska Women's History

American Quilt Study Group
35th and Holdrege St.
East Campus Loop
Po Box 4737
Lincoln, NE 68504-0737

Nebraska Historical Society
1500 R St.
PO Box 82554
Lincoln, NE 68501-2553

Special Collections, University of Nebraska
308 Love Library
Lincoln, NE 68588-0333

Common Nebraska Surnames

The following surnames are among the most common in Nebraska and are also being currently researched by other genealogists. If you find your surname here, there is a chance that some research has already been performed on your ancestor.

Adams, Antelope, Arthur, Banner, Blaine, Boone, Box, Butte, Boyd, Brown, Buffalo, Burt, Butle, Cass, Cedar, Chase, Cherry, Cheyenne, Clay, Colfax, Cuming, Custer, Dakota, Dawes, Dawson, Deuel, Dixon, Dodge, Douglas, Dundy, Fillmore, Franklin, Frontier, Furnas, Gage, Garden, Garfield, Gosper, Grant, Greeley, Hall, Hamilton, Harlan, Hayes, Hitchcock, Holt, Hooker, Howard, Jefferson, Johnson, Kearney, Keith, Keya Paha, Kimball, Knox, Lancaster, Lincoln, Logan, Loup, Madison, McPherson, Merrick, Morrill, Nance, Nemaha, Nuckolls, Otoe, Pawnee, Perkins, Phelps, Pierce, Platte, Polk, Red Willow, Richardson, Rock, Saline, Sarpy, Saunders, Scotts Bluff, Seward, Sheridan, Sherman, Sioux, Stanton, Thayer, Thomas, Thurston, Valley, Washington, Wayne, Webster, Wheeler, York

About the Author

Gary L. Morris worked from 2009 to 2014 as a professional researcher for a major player in the genealogy field. After tracing his family lineage back to 1683, he found that genealogy could be an expensive undertaking. As such, has decided to publish these helpful guides to share the valuable free information he has discovered during his career to help others trace their family lineages as inexpensively as possible. An avid genealogist himself, he hopes you will find this guide factual, thorough, helpful, and most of all, effective in helping you to find your family members.

Notes

Notes

www.ingramcontent.com/pod-product-compliance
Lightning Source LLC
Chambersburg PA
CBHW070517290526
45790CB00003B/1247